A Wing and a Prayer

By Franklin Graham

Illustrated by Kevin Burke

Tommy NELSON®

www.tommynelson.com

A Division of Thomas Nelson, Inc.
www.ThomasNelson.com

Text © 2005 by Franklin Graham
Illustrations © 2005 by Tommy Nelson®

Published in Nashville, Tennessee, by Tommy Nelson®, a Division of Thomas Nelson, Inc.

Tommy Nelson® books may be purchased in bulk for educational, business, fundraising, or sales
promotion use. For information, please e-mail SpecialMarkets@Thomas Nelson.com

Library of Congress Cataloging-in-Publication Data

Graham, Franklin, 1952-
A wing and a prayer / by Franklin Graham ; illustrated by Kevin Burke.
p. cm.
Summary: Raimundo, an eight-year-old boy living in a jungle village, has not spoken since his parents were
killed a year earlier, but a special box filled by a new friend in America helps to transform his life.

ISBN 1-4003-0114-9 (hardcover)
[1. Charity—Fiction. 2. Christian life—Fiction. 3. Missionaries—Fiction. 4. Orphans—Fiction.
5. Christmas—Fiction.] I. Burke, Kevin, 1969- ill. II. Title.

PZ7.G751675Wi 2005
[Fic]—dc22

2005006390

Printed in the United States of America
05 06 07 08 — 5 4 3 2 1

Dear Reader,

I have had the opportunity of working with children all over the world. As you read this book, I hope that God will speak to your heart because He loves and cares for you. He has shown this by sending His Son out of heaven to offer you the greatest gift of all—salvation from sin. If you had been the *only* person ever to live in all of history, Jesus Christ would have come to this earth just for you. That is how important you are to Him. Whether you are rich or poor, black, white, brown, or red, you are unique with a personality all your own.

Living the Christian life is an exciting adventure. I pray that you will discover God's plan and purpose for your life through faith in His Son, the Lord Jesus Christ, just as Raimundo does in this story you are about to read. I hope that you will pray and ask Him to show you what He has planned for your life.

God bless you,

Franklin Graham

Jesse had just put the finishing touches on his shoebox. With a smile, he walked to the front of his class and stacked his box among the others. The teacher began to pray:

> Dear Jesus, please find special kids to receive all
> these Christmas presents. Help this to be the
> best Christmas they have ever had. Help them
> to know that You love them like You love us.

As the children put away their wrapping paper and tape, crayons and stickers, Jesse's teacher explained how each shoebox would complete an amazing journey. Each box would travel around the world until it found its way to a child needing to hear of God's love.

That night, as Jesse crawled into bed, he wondered about the little boy who would open his shoebox.

Raimundo, an eight-year-old boy, had no idea that Christmas was about to come to Alto Riesgo. In his poor, tiny village that lay deep in the jungle, March was a hot and sticky time of year. Raimundo had never been anywhere else in the whole world, and rarely had anyone come to visit the isolated village.

But Raimundo clearly remembered the day that Dr. Annie came from America. She brought medicine for the sick and even helped the villagers learn to speak English. The children taught her how to make round balls from the river mud, and she taught them how to play soccer with a ball she had given to them.

For Raimundo, however, there was no fun in this village. He usually just watched the other children jump rope and play soccer. He missed his parents and feared that the men with the guns would return—the men who took his parents away.

"Hi, Raimundo." Sarita smiled and sat down next to him. "Do you like my dolly? Her name is Esperanza. It means *hope*. I pray that God will give you hope and make you smile again." But Sarita couldn't make his frown disappear.

From off in the distance, a buzzing noise grew louder. All the children stopped playing, ran into the open, and looked into the blue sky. Pedro began jumping up and down. Manuel screeched with excitement. "An airplane!"

Dr. Annie huddled the children close together as the plane circled the village and then safely landed on the grass strip. When the pilot opened the door, Dr. Annie and the children saw their friend Mateo hop down as the dust swirled around his feet. "Merry Christmas!" he shouted over the roar of the engine.

"Christmas?" Annie asked. "What are you talking about, Mateo?"

Just then, Dan Hogan, the pilot, unlatched the cargo door of the small plane. The children ran, nearly stumbling over each other, and peered into the airplane. Brightly colored boxes were stacked all the way to the top.

"Merry Christmas!" Mateo shouted. "Build a fire! Fry some tortillas! We're having a fiesta tonight!"

As the sun set behind the big palms, Mateo explained his surprise visit.

"This is a special time for all of us," Mateo explained, looking into the hopeful faces of the kids. "Children in the United States, a country far away, decided to celebrate Christmas by giving something to you. Christmas is the time when God sent His only Son to earth to give us hope. Jesus is the greatest gift ever given to anyone."

Dr. Annie, Mateo, and Dan handed out the boxes. "On the count of three," Mateo shouted, "you can rip them open."

"Uno,

Dos,

Tres!"

"Tres" was drowned out by the happy squeals of the children, as wrapping paper was tossed into the warm, night air.

As the children played show-and-tell with their presents, Dan noticed a somber little boy sitting alone. Dan nudged Annie. "What's with him?"

Annie looked up at Raimundo. "His parents were killed in a village raid last year. He hasn't spoken since."

Dan walked over to the dwindling pile of shoeboxes and picked up an oversized box marked "BOY." Dan slowly approached Raimundo and held the box up for him.

Raimundo just shook his head.

"No?" Dan asked. "Somebody very special packed this box for you. Who knows? Maybe you'll make a new friend if you accept this gift."

Raimundo turned away, his lip quivering.

Dan raised the lid of the box. He whistled. "Wow!"

With a little curiosity, Raimundo looked over. To his surprise, Dan was pumping up a soccer ball. He held out the ball until Raimundo reached for it.

"Now that wasn't so hard, was it?" Dan asked with a smile. He held the box up. "Why don't you see what else is in there?"

Raimundo carefully examined each of the items: a harmonica, a toy motorcycle, a bookmark with a Bible verse, a toothbrush. Dan began to show Raimundo all the things you *should not* do with a toothbrush—comb your hair, scratch your back—and, to Dan's surprise, the sad, little boy's frown turned into giggles.

Finally, Raimundo reached into the box and pulled out a round object wrapped in string. He held it up to Dan and shrugged his shoulders.

"Amigo, that's a yo-yo!" Dan answered. "Here, let me show you how it works."

Dan put his finger through the loop and propelled it through the air. Raimundo's eyes widened. Dan handed the yo-yo to Raimundo, helping him lace his finger through the string.

The lesson was interrupted when they heard Annie call out, "Dan . . . Raimundo, the tortillas are almost done. It's time to celebrate!"

As Raimundo put all the gifts back into the box, he saw an envelope. Raimundo grabbed it and shoved it into Dan's hand.

"Oh," Dan said, "this is a letter to you."

Dan slowly read each word to him.

To my new friend,

Merry Christmas! This shoebox is packed just for YOU. I live in an orphanage with lots of other kids, but I am going to live with a nice family soon.

I hope you like all this stuff. I prayed that it would help make you happy. The yo-yo is my favorite. Mr. Peters (my new dad) said that the yo-yo is sort of like Jesus. He came to earth to save us, went up to heaven to make a home for us, and one day, will return to earth to take us to heaven with Him. He came and left and will come back again—just like the yo-yo.

It's so much fun to have a new friend so far away. I'm praying for you. I'll check the mail every day looking for a letter from you.

Your new friend,
Jesse

P.S. Draw me a picture of you with the yo-yo

The morning after the celebration, Raimundo sat at the base of a banana tree. The sun's rays, beaming through the branches, sparked memories of Raimundo and his father. He remembered shimmying up the trunks of the trees and throwing bunches of bananas down to his padre. He wished for times like that again.

Raimundo's thoughts were interrupted when Pedro pulled at his arm. "I'll let you listen to my new CD player if you'll let us play with your soccer ball."

Raimundo kicked the ball toward Pedro.

"Thanks, amigo." Pedro threw the ball to his friends, and Manuel kicked it so hard that it flew right past Raimundo. Raimundo took off, chasing the ball toward the line of trees and shrubs just beyond the village.

Annie rushed up behind Dan, breathless. "Dan, stop him! We're afraid the men who attacked the village are camped just beyond those trees. If they see Raimundo . . ."

"Raimundo!" Dan shouted. "Stop!"

But Raimundo continued to chase the ball. Dan followed. Just as Raimundo reached the ball, Dan grabbed him and slung him onto his shoulders.

When they returned to the field where the kids were playing, Raimundo couldn't believe his ears.

"Raimundo! Way to go! You saved our ball!" They were all cheering for him!

Raimundo smiled, holding the ball way up in the air before tossing it down to all the children looking up at him.

Dr. Annie leaned toward Dan. "That was too close," she whispered.

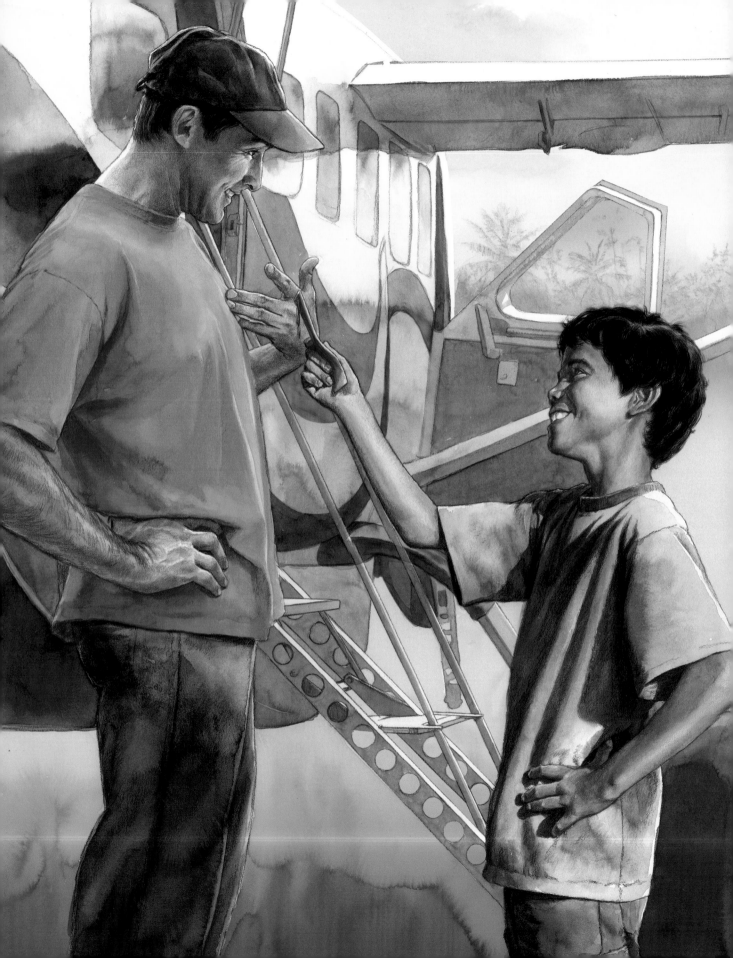

Later that day, Dr. Annie, Dan, and Mateo talked with the chief of the village. Annie sat down with the children and explained, "It is not safe for us to stay here. It's only a matter of time before the men who attacked the village come again. We need to leave this village quickly."

As Raimundo gathered his things, he found the bookmark that Jesse had sent in his box of surprises. Raimundo smiled and handed it to Dan. "W-would you help me read these words that Jesse sent to me?"

With great surprise, Dan turned and looked at the boy. "Raimundo, you can talk!" He picked him up and swung him around. "Of course, I will!"

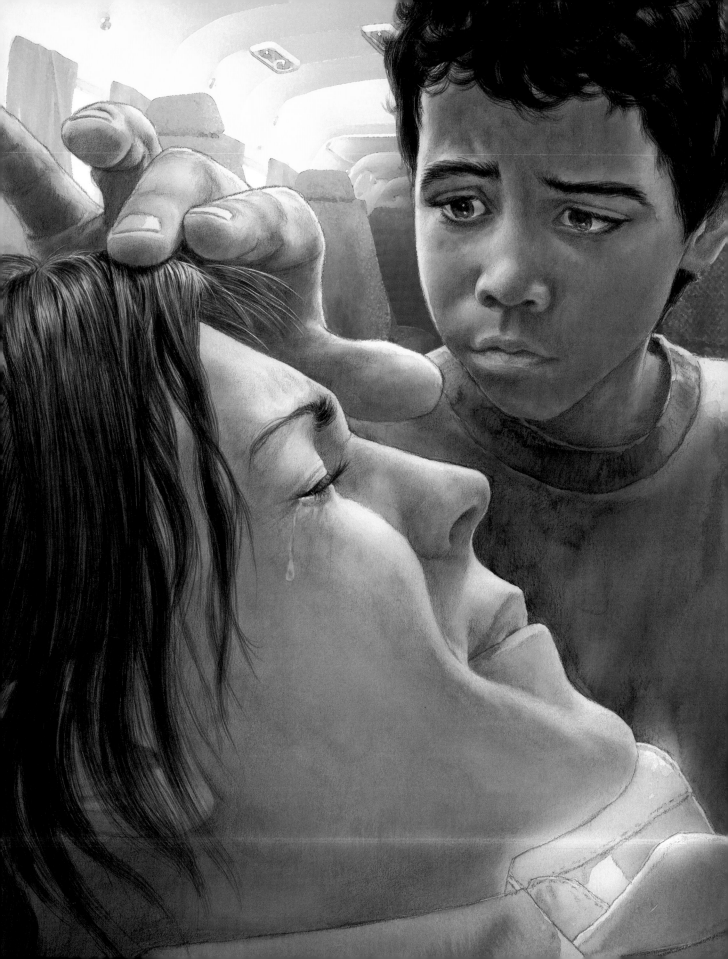

After the plane was loaded and the villagers were safely on board, Dan brought the engine to a roar. The plane began rumbling over the rough, rocky ground, speeding faster and faster until the plane's wheels were in the air. The villagers watched Alto Riesgo, and the danger that surrounded it, grow further and further away from them.

As Dan directed the plane over a row of trees, he saw several men running toward the plane. "Stay down!" he yelled to his passengers.

Raimundo heard a popping noise as he peered through the windows. The men with guns were shooting at them and had hit a wing of the plane! Struggling, Dan regained control and tried to guide the plane to climb higher.

Dr. Annie was making her way from the cockpit toward the children when she suddenly fell to the floor of the plane, clutching her arm. She had been hit. The children screamed—all but Raimundo. He crawled over to Dr. Annie, stroked her forehead, and whispered a prayer: "Please, God, save Dr. Annie. Please save Dr. Annie and get us to our new home."

The children peered through the windows as the trees became smaller. Raimundo looked up into the clouds and wondered if he was closer to God. Soon after, on one good wing and a whispered prayer, the small plane full of villagers glided home to safety.

As they touched down, Dan called out, "Here we are, children—your new home!"

When the plane rolled to a stop, the villagers stepped out onto Villa Placida, meaning *peaceful village*. A doctor and nurse were there to meet them, and they whisked Dr. Annie off in an ambulance to a missionary hospital.

Seeing the frightened look on Raimundo's face, Dan leaned over and said, "Dr. Annie's going to be just fine. Would you like to go to the hospital with me to check on her?"

"Can we? Can we?" Raimundo asked.

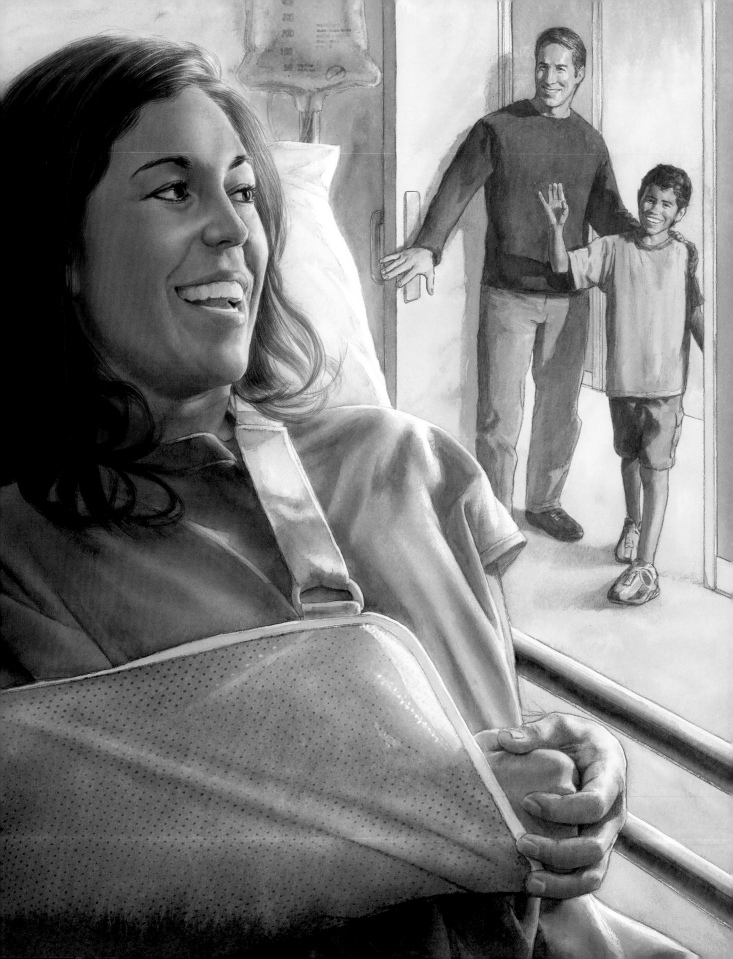

Dan and Raimundo climbed up into an old truck parked next to the plane and bounced over the rough trails until they came to a little hospital. After a long wait in the courtyard, the nurse told Dan and Raimundo they could see Dr. Annie.

"Señor Dan saved us from the men with the guns!" Raimundo exclaimed as soon as they entered the room.

Dr. Annie smiled and calmly replied, "Raimundo, remember the Bible verse we all learned? Proverbs 3:5–6: 'Trust in the LORD with all your heart, . . . and He shall direct your paths.' Jesus is with us, Raimundo. He is the One who saves."

Raimundo smiled and nodded. "Tell me more about Him, Dr. Annie. Tell me more. I want to know Jesus the way that you and Señor Dan do."

Dr. Annie glanced at Dan through tearful eyes, knowing that God had answered their prayers. Dan looked up at Annie and then knelt down beside Raimundo. "If you believe in Jesus with all your heart, Raimundo, say this prayer with me:

> Dear Jesus,
> Please help me to trust You to keep me safe in
> Your hands. Please forgive me for everything I've
> done wrong. Come into my heart and help me to
> be better and help me to do what You want me
> to do. Amen.

Raimundo thought about each word as he repeated after Dan. Then he added, "And thank you for my friends, Dr. Annie, Señor Dan, and my new friend, Jesse."

"Raimundo . . ." Dan put his hand on Raimundo's shoulder. "We have something special to tell you. Dr. Annie and I are going to be married in a few days."

Raimundo quickly looked to the floor.

"Why the frown?" Dr. Annie asked.

Raimundo didn't look up. "Are you going to leave us?"

"Raimundo, how can we go away and leave all of the friends that we love?" Annie began. "God has called us to live here and has provided for all of our needs. But we've also asked the Lord for something very special. Do you know what it is?"

Raimundo's eyes lit up. "A shoebox of surprises?"

"No, Raimundo," Dan said with a grin. "We've asked the Lord to give us a son, just like you. We know your parents will always be in your heart. But would you like to live with us and let us take care of you?"

Raimundo tried to speak, but the words just wouldn't come.

"You don't have to answer us right now, Raimundo, just think about it."

To my new friend, Jesse,

Thank you for giving me the best Christmas ever. You gave me the most fun gifts and the best surprises.

I'm sharing my soccer ball with Manuel and Pedro, and every time I spin my yo-yo, I think of how Jesus left heaven and came to earth to give me the best gift ever, then returned to heaven to make a home for me there some day. He came and went back, just like my yo-yo.

And guess what else? Jesus gave me a new home, just like you. I live with Señor Dan and Dr. Annie in a safe village. I've learned that no matter where I am, Jesus will always keep me safe.

I did what you asked and drew a picture of me with the yo-yo. Maybe we'll meet some day. . . .

Your new friend,
Raimundo

P.S. I memorized the Bible verse. Here is one for you:
"There is a friend who sticks closer than a brother."
Proverbs 18:24

If you would like to receive the bookmark
"The Gospel Alphabet" please write:

Samaritan's Purse
P. O. Box 3000
Boone, NC 28607